PSYCHEDELIC PSALMS

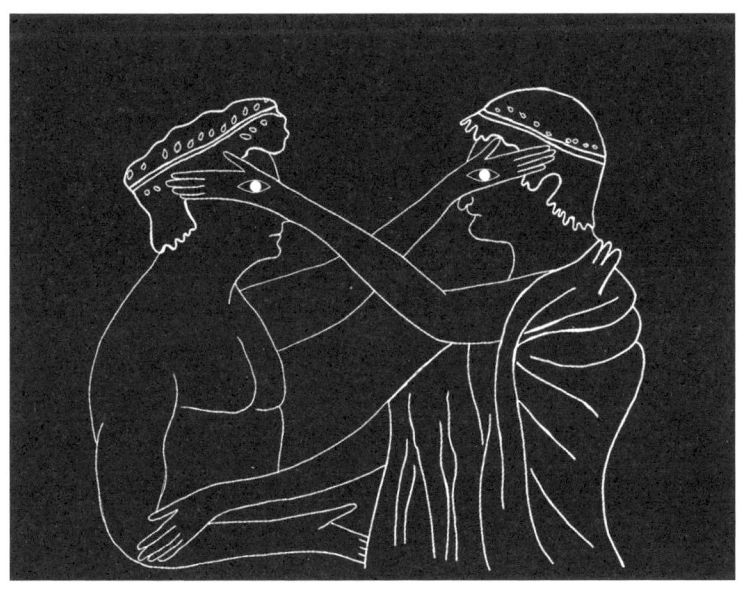

By Joshua Dean Rogers

Illustrations by Mariano Chavez

HAT & BEARD PRESS | LOS ANGELES

This book is dedicated to my brother Jeff, who died too young.

I will find you out there in the Universe brother.

We will sit on the floor together and listen to KISS records once again.

Our circle will be unbroken.

To G.A. and V.K.—thank you for waking me up.

What are poets for in such an age? What is the use of poetry? The state of the world calls out for poetry to save it.

If you would be a poet, create works capable of answering the challenge of these apocalyptic times. Even if it means sounding apocalyptic.

...you can conquer the conquerors with words.

If you would be a poet, write living newspapers. Be a reporter from outer space, filing dispatches to some Supreme Managing Editor who believes in full disclosure and has a low tolerance for bullshit.

—Lawrence Ferlinghetti

Poetry As Insurgent Art, 1975

Satori:

Japanese for Sudden Enlightenment.

First thought = best thought.

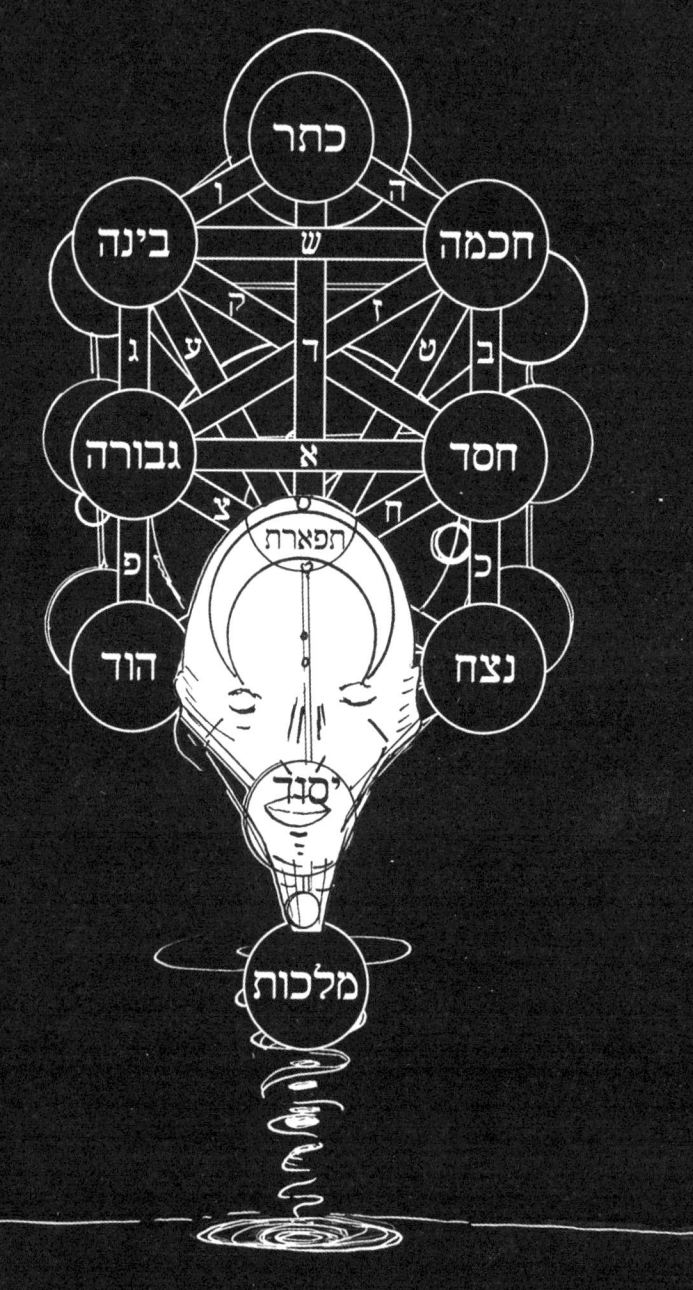

Kabbalah Meditations

In what ways am I using the "I want"?
Am I not connecting to the Source?

My Mantra—I AM the Source, I don't *need* anything.

The container will never be full enough:
It always wants more.

What can I give the other person?
What does the other person need?

Don't get excited when things go well and go back to "I need."

When I am the Source, I know that I am bringing something unique and valuable to the other person. Then I awaken the Source in them.
Light awakens light.

What we are missing most in life is clarity.

Humiliate myself.

Hug strangers randomly.

Immerse myself in water while meditating on washing away old behaviors.

Stay up all night while studying something spiritual.

Choose twelve waking hours and do not speak at all.

Ask the Light for a vision of what my soul's potential is.

Once I acknowledge how faraway I am, I will receive the light I need to get to my true potential.

Less thinking and more doing will reveal more Light.

Gather up all the energy I've misplaced in tasks or activities that have no higher value or only served myself.

The Goal of Life: to come into the world as one person and transform into the perfected version of myself.

The Game of Life

Everything I'm about to say has already been said.
But not by me.
And not at this time, and not in this way.

How many times does a message need to be repeated?
For a child (or an adult) to internalize the message?
Clearly the answer must be...
thousands of times,
over thousands of years.
Thousands of incarnations,
told by a hundred sages.
And so here it is again...
Same story, different messenger:

Life is indeed an epic game
that each of us chooses
over and over again:
the wheel of karma,
the wheel of birth and rebirth
To make the game more interesting
we drink from the river of forgetfulness
before dropping in...

Why did Neem Karoli Baba laugh and smile so much?
Because he was already in the winner's circle,
just enjoying the divine comedy,
watching the rest of us stumble
and bumble our way along the game board.
It is rather comic, but in a loving way.

"All the world is a stage, and we are merely players upon it."
—a theater, a film, an epic comedy.
God said, "Lights, camera, action!"
(This could have been the first line of Genesis)
And the Game began.
Think something like "Chutes and Ladders," but for the soul.
Each of us is a player.

So many cynics have intuited the comedy of the game.
But they did not see clearly.
They concluded falsely that the game has no meaning.
Slide back ten spaces!

All of those depressing Frenchmen...
Dour Derrida
Cynical Sartre
Campy Camus
Foppish Foucault
Each of them souring the mood of an entire century.

You too Mr. T.S. Eliot!
Slide back 10 spaces.
Your *Wasteland* wasted an entire generation.

The Game does have a purpose.
We come into each lifetime as one person
We must transform into the perfected version of ourselves.
That is how we advance along the game board.
The Game does have a purpose.
In each lifetime we must correct our tikkun,
correct our karma.
correct the world.

Tikkun Olam

Advance 10 spaces.
The Game does have a purpose.
We must walk each other home
to God
We must learn to love…
everybody
Advance more spaces.
The Game does have a purpose.
We have to learn that we are all the same.
We have to learn to forgive…
everybody
The Game does have a purpose.
When we create we are acting like God.
We just have to Remember
what we already know in our immortal souls.
Remember:
The Game does have a purpose.
But there are no winners until we all make it home.
The Big Bang was the beginning,
an explosion of souls
separated
The goal of the game is for all of us to reunite.
Where we are all once again
One.

That's when the "whirligig of time" stops.

Hence this famous prayer
that says it all:
Shema Yisrael
Adonai eloheinu
Adonai echad.
Hear O Israel!
The Eternal One is our God,
The Eternal One is **Oneness**.

Everything I have said has already been said.
But not by me.
And not at this time, and not in this way.

If You're Not Crying to Some Music, You're Not Deeply Listening

Close your eyes. Let the music wash over you.

Let the music vibrate in your whole body.

If you really focus on the music, the beauty and emotion of it will stir your soul.

These works are of such stunning beauty:

- Rachmaninov *Symphony No. 2 3rd Movement Adagio*
- Max Bruch *Kol Nidre Opus 47*
- Beethoven *Piano Concerto No. 5 2nd Movement Adagio un poco moto*
- Palestrina *Sicut Cervus*
- Lee Morgan *Since I Fell For You*

The Necessity of Forgiveness

Forgiveness must become a paramount virtue today. Forgiveness is essential to the possibility and survival of a civil society.

The backlash against "wokeness" is justified insofar as there is currently a zero-forgiveness policy from the extreme left. Just as we cannot blame a German born after WWII for the Holocaust, so too must we stop blaming today's whites for the sins of slavery, or today's young men for the sins of misogyny. We must simultaneously acknowledge and never forget those past sins and yet we must forgive and move on.

Because all humans are fallible, we must forgive or else we will devolve into a hellish Hobbesian state of nature. Forgiveness starts with the recognition of our own individual fallibility. What is most objectionable about the extreme left's woke policing and cancel culture is the false self-righteousness. Who among us has not said the wrong thing at the wrong time? Who among us has not held an unfair stereotype in our minds? The pendulum must swing back to moderation and a tolerance for mistakes and occasionally boorish behavior.

Without forgiveness, culture wars will quickly devolve into actual civil wars.

Just because I disagree with you does not mean that I hate you. This must be re-learned by the whole society or else there is no hope for a democratic republic.

Forgiveness was Jesus' most important teaching.

On Victimhood and Power

Victimhood is not a virtue. Power is not necessarily unjust.

Today, we live in a time of the Victimhood Olympics. Being a victim, identifying oneself as being part of a victimized identity group, is now wielded as an asset. Being a victim never has and never will be a true asset. Part of the objective of life is to pull oneself out of being a victim of anyone or anything.

Having power does not make a person or a nation inherently unjust. Having power means having responsibility to be just and virtuous in the wielding of power. Power used rightly has the potential to help all humanity evolve and get closer to God.

Humans (particularly in the United States at this time) must evolve past this phase. This current behavior is utterly juvenile. It is the behavior of an immature and entitled teenager who thinks that the world should be made perfectly just and equitable for them.

No one really believes in equality anyway. People only want "equality" with those they perceive to have *more* than themselves. But no one wants to be equal to those that have *less* than themselves. The cry for "equality" is pure hypocrisy. The Game of Life does not work this way.

Inoculating the Youth from the Most Worrisome Epidemic—Technology Sickness

We are living inside an Infosphere. We cannot discern the difference between information and knowledge. They soon will not be able to discern inside the Infosphere who is human and who is AI. Loneliness and confusion are an epidemic among the youth. Education can be like an inoculation for the youth from the dangers of technology. But the pedagogy must be to physically remove them from the Infosphere for a period of four years. They must go to a technology-free retreat—a monastery in the mountains where they only interact with books, one another, and teachers only face-to-face. Only through a combination of solitude, intense reading, learning how to discuss and evaluate ideas face-to-face and how to socialize can the youth be taught how to eventually deal effectively with the technology, but also how to make sound judgments and how to think for themselves—in short how to be fully human.

The cure for technology loneliness is to get the youth off their phones and off all technology for a spell. It will take a full four years of face-to-face interaction mixed with solitude and plenty of reading the great books (of all cultures) in order to train them how to be human.

Many adults will see this cure and they will flock to cure themselves as well. The ideal educational institution of the now and the future will be a place for all ages. Education is a lifelong pursuit.

On Photography

Photography is the product of complete alienation.

—Marcel Proust

Using technology, as opposed to the human hand, to create art is another form of alienation or abstraction from our own humanity.

The Ants and the Owls

Once upon a time there was a colony of ants. The ants were mostly very industrious. In fact, generations of ants, thanks to their focus on gathering sticks, had fashioned a very nice colony for themselves replete with all the finest sticks that nature can produce. Their colony had so many luxuries that the older ants were very aware of how easy the young ants had it compared to generations before. The ants were convinced that their approach to education and work were the key to the success of their colony. You see, the ants believed that each ant had a role to play in the colony. Some ants were diggers, some were scouts for sticks, some were stick carriers, some were leaf carriers, others were architects of the ant hill, and so on. There were so many different roles within the colony. Since each ant would spend his whole adult life working in his role until he died, it was important to train the ants when they were young for their eventual roles. Therefore, the purpose of school for the ants was strictly to prepare them for their vocations. The school in the colony had departments for each job—the department of ant hill architecture, the department of leaf scouting, and so forth. In the old days, the young ants got assigned to their departments in school based on what roles their parents and grandparents did during their lives. But a few generations ago, this particular ant colony had a few very progressive leaders that had heard through the grapevine of something that owls did. It was a radical concept: that young ants should be allowed to choose (regardless of their family history) what department they would be schooled and ultimately work in. Despite this radical notion, for most young ants, their parents basically decided for them anyway. Plus, since the ant parents had to pay a portion of their fruit supplies to the ant school, they were very focused on making sure their young got the necessary certifications to ensure they would have a role in the colony.

And so, the ants continued this way of life and education. They were so busy working in their roles and acquiring more sticks and eating more fruits and vegetables. As far as the ants were concerned, there wasn't really anything else to life other than working, eating, and reproducing. The ants didn't think it was very "useful" to allow their young to read, discuss, or think about any questions other than learning how to do their eventual jobs. Everything worked fine for the ant colony so long as they had a good and wise Queen Ant in charge. It should also be noted how the ants felt about their lives—to the extent they did any thinking at all. The ants had all the food and sticks any ant could want, and yet all the ants in the colony still felt a never-ending hunger and boredom. When the ants had a few quiet moments to actually think, they couldn't stand it—immediately they would busy themselves with some other diversion, or more work, or more consuming of food, or chasing more leaves and sticks. In the old days, the ants would talk to each other about how they felt, but recently they took to "clicking" each other which involved knocking their antennae together in a code. All the clicking in the colony suggested that the ants were really very unhappy with life, but they didn't know how to change it.

And then one day, the good and wise Queen Ant died.

The new Queen Ant II had a very different plan for the colony. Queen Ant II knew that all the ants only cared about working, eating, reproducing, and watching ant sports on the weekends. As long as she made sure they had those basics, she could steal all the other resources of the colony for herself and her small group of friends. The ants would never question anything. She also knew that there was certain small minority group of ants that she didn't like because they had longer antennae than the rest of the colony, including her small cadre of friends. She would just kill them off in a quick little genocide using the ant troops at her disposal. The other ants wouldn't care, after all, it wasn't in their nature to question anything. Plus, they only knew about the latest ant celebrities. Queen Ant II executed all her plans with no difficulty and no resistance.

And so, the ants continued in this way of life and education. The ants in the colony didn't even realize that they were slaves. And they were unhappy. Then their whole colony died a few years later because they didn't realize that they had consumed all the food in their immediate area. But at least their methods of education were "useful."

◊

Once upon a time, there was a community (Parliament) of owls. The owls, like the ants, were also industrious. Like the ants, they had many of the same concerns: food, shelter, working, reproducing, etc. But the owls had the advantage of flight. The owls knew that the world was huge, beautiful, and mysterious. Because of this, the owls were naturally curious. They wanted to know more about this world. Now, the owls also had selfish and jealous ones among them. The owls knew, through an ancient oral tradition of stories, that past owls had lived as slaves under selfish tyrants. They had also lived in past generations in systems where some owls were given the choicest trees based only on the color of their feathers. Correspondingly, the education of young owls in old times was basically the same as the education systems that the ants practiced. Young owls in the old days were trained specifically for the roles they would play in the owl community: nest-making technologies, rodent kinesiology, hunting in low moonlight situations, and so forth. But a few generations ago, sick of so many years of the traditional ways of organizing owl communities that created injustice and sorrow for the majority of owls, a few wise elder owls decided to start a new community founded on a radical idea. The idea was essentially that owls were capable of organizing their community without a King Owl in charge and with equal opportunity for all owls regardless of feather color, beak shape, or forest of origination. But in order for this to work, there was a critical lynchpin: the young owls would need to spend a few years (when they were old enough to join the community) being educated on how to think for themselves. This had to happen before they could focus on their vocation. The young owls were taught by the wisest of the older owls and the most curious among them. The teacher owls did not lecture though (after all, the wise owls were still learners themselves and knew that they did not know all the answers). One of the goals of the education was to help the young owls learn how to ask good questions. Another was how to talk amongst themselves after hearing all the stories of the wisest owls who have ever lived. The young owls would learn what the wisest owls have said about the mysteries of life, how the world works, and what they had observed from owl communities in many different forests. During these few short years before they went into a vocation, the young owls would discuss and argue amongst themselves about their teachers' ideas, such as justice, virtue, and beauty. Even though the young owls had different opinions, they learned how to listen to other owls carefully and respectfully without pecking each other's eyes out. They learned how to compromise with each other, and they learned that sometimes their own opinion wasn't as thoroughly examined as they thought it was. The young owls learned how to use and respect the one owl principle that make it possible for the owls to govern themselves: reason.

After the young owls were done with this mandatory education, they were then free to choose whatever vocation they wished. They then trained in those vocations and took their place in the community as hunters, nest-builders, etc. Since the owls respected reason and loved learning and discussing ideas, if they were ever asked by their fellow owls to represent them in the council of owl leaders, they were capable and happy to serve with the same equanimity and respect for all owls, regardless of their views, as they had when they were in their "Owl Citizen School" years. Additionally, since all the owls were educated in this manner, they knew how to evaluate an argument and they could tell if a leader was lying to them. If a leader was selfish or unjust, all the owls would simply vote him out of the leadership council.

And so, the owls were able to govern themselves without having to hope that a King or Queen was good and wise. The owls never lived as slaves again. The owls had equal opportunity for all because of their universal respect for reason and justice. They were able to compromise with each other and resolve differences because they knew how to talk to each other respectfully. And using reason as an arbiter, they could decide which arguments had greater merit. The owls' curiosity and love of learning and discussing ideas also made them more keenly aware to their environment and the condition of their forests. They noticed the interdependency of all living things on the earth. And they recognized how to live in harmony with nature. All of this was accomplished because of the owls' recognition of these principles and their method of education, which the ants would see as "useless."

And this is why owls live long lives, are happy, and wise.

I walk through the market of life, and I am neither a buyer nor a seller.

—Neem Karoli Baba, known as the Maharajji

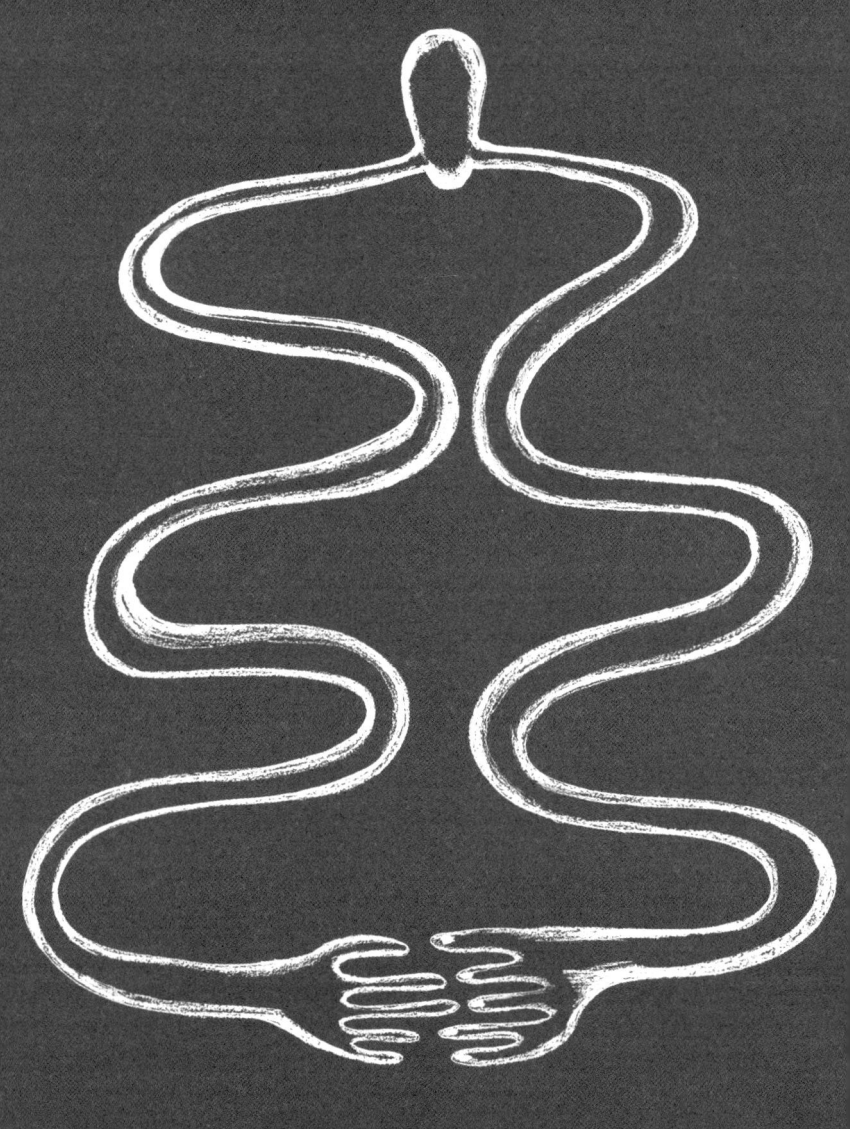

Darkness is the Source

The deep dark center of the pyramids is related to the darkness that Lao Tzu thought was the beginning of the potentiality for Light.

The beginning of immortality is the darkness of the New Moon in the lunar cycle.

The voice of God is always in music that is deep, dark, and low.

Musical accompaniment to this aphorism—listen to "Time" by Hans Zimmer.

"Would you relax? They never look up."

Abstraction from Ourselves and Others

We now conduct warfare from what is essentially a video gaming room.

We use robotic machines to do our killing for us.

We don't hear the cries of agony or feel the warm blood of our enemy on our skin.

If we felt the visceral nature of killing, we wouldn't be so quick to do it over and over again.

Lack of human connection leads to a lack of consequences.

All of modernity is abstraction. That's why people in Brooklyn are raising chickens on their roof in response.

"The path to the Truth is to bring people to the table to talk."
—Thomas Reid, *Common Sense*

We don't even know how to handwrite a letter anymore.

Hand + pen + paper is a visceral experience that requires effort and a little bit of love and respect for the recipient.

Technology will reach a point where hopefully it facilitates authentic conversation bringing in more viewpoints/experience from across the universe—fingers crossed.

Open Up My Chest

I have a big "S" for "Super Love" under my chest

Walk around and just beam it like a spotlight

Superman symbol = Super Love

Pull open my rib cage

Golden rays shining out of my chest

Formulas for Happiness

Happiness = Wanting what you have

÷ Having what you want

Happiness = Gratitude ÷ Gratification

Anxiety = Uncertainty x Powerlessness

Progress + Personal Growth = Happiness

Is it Worth It?

Ask if everything I do each day is in alignment with who I want to be?

Return daily to my core principles and my goals.

It's not how well you play the game; it's about deciding what kind of game you want to play.

People are so focused on the length of life, but what about the width, quality and depth of moments?

On the Key to Life

Find someplace that you love and make it better.

—Eva Brann (Former Dean of St. John's College, Annapolis)

Inform, Invite, Introduce

Do one of these things for all people you encounter.

Five Biggest Regrets People Have Before They Die

1. I wish I pursued my dreams and aspirations, and not the life others expected of me.

2. I wish I didn't work so hard.

3. I wish I had the courage to express my feelings and speak my mind.

4. I wish I had stayed in touch with my friends.

5. I wish I had let myself be happier.

Scary vs. Dangerous

Repelling off a cliff is scary, but the rope you are harnessed to can hold a car. So, in fact, it's not dangerous.

Staying in a job that you will regret your whole life, or hiking on a snowy mountain in May when it's beautiful out, are both not scary. In fact, they are extremely dangerous (regret and avalanche).

It's critical to make the distinction between scary and dangerous.

Strong vs. Tough

Most of my life, I thought toughness was a masculine virtue. But my wife set me straight. When someone says of a co-worker that they are "tough" to deal with, that is not referring to a virtue. Toughness refers to a certain irascibility. Toughness suggests insensibility. My father can easily withstand a needle to the eyeball. Maybe that is not necessarily a virtue in itself.

When people say someone is "strong", they never mean that negatively. Strength is always considered a virtue. To be strong, however, does not mean to not feel things. In fact, quite the opposite. Strength is only true strength when you feel pain and loss and empathy, and yet somehow you overcome and persevere.

Strive for strength, not toughness.

Too Much Lecturing, Not Enough Reading and Talking Together

All these gurus are just lecturing to you.
We do not learn or really internalize anything
when we are passive and merely receiving.

Just as one memorizes better by handwriting,
so too must we read books actively and
then discuss them together
with the guru along with all the other learners and seekers.

True learning happens from
private
personal
active engagement with a text
and then again around a seminar table,
not in a lecture hall or a giant auditorium.

This is what all the previous gurus have misunderstood.

The method must be small
face-to-face groups
talking to each other
about the same book, art, or music.

On Baldness—You Make the Connection

Buddhist monks
Jean Luc Picard/Patrick Stewart
Steven Covey
Michael Pollan
Jeffrey Katzenberg
Pope Francis
Bryan Cranston
Kobe Bryant
Samuel L. Jackson
Jeff Bezos
Michael Jordan
Dalai Lama
Mahatma Gandhi
Socrates
Pablo Picasso
Mark Rothko
Arnold Schoenberg
Lawrence Ferlinghetti
Ram Dass
Allen Ginsberg
Shel Silverstein
Dogen
Sigmund Freud
Albert Hoffman
James Fadiman
Kingsley Price
Seneca
Neem Karoli Baba — The Maharajji
G.W. Leibniz
Rick Rubin
Yuval Noah Harari
Lao Tzu
William Blake
Jackson Pollock
Seth Godin
Paulo Coelho
Peter Attia
Leon Botstein
Daniel Quinn
Leon Golub
Rabbi Steve Leder
Mark Nepo

The Best Aspects of All World Religions

They are all attempting to describe the same thing.
Everyone is seeking the Truth.

Divinity schools and medical schools and
philosophy schools are all coming
together and merging.

Psychology, ethno-botany, philosophy,
medicine, theology, art—all merging together.

We are evolving toward a collective understanding of the
"Varieties of Religious Experience", as William James called it.

Be Like Water

Forty-eight years through this lifetime
Maybe I'm getting wiser
You can't begin to understand the Tao
In youth when the Ego is in full bloom
"Strength" is an illusion
To be "strong as a rock" is to be dumb as a rock
The strongest force on this planet is also the weakest
Water bends and conforms
Water sustains and refreshes all who drink it
Water is a servant to all life
When rocks and trees fall in its way
Water does not complain
Water simply flows around, above, and below all obstructions
Water can bore a hole into rock
Rock is powerless to the gentle persistence of water
I must be like water
The Way of Virtue is to be like water
Water does not expect anything from anything else
I too must not expect anything from anyone
Water submits and accepts
Yet water has a quiet profound power
The beauty of a gently babbling brook in the mountains
Meandering through the trees
The soothing sound of that flowing trickle of water in the summer
The deep silence while standing on the snow above the creek in winter
The flowing trickle. . . and the silence
Together
Oneness
Flow
My soul is home

Passing Over

Passing Over to immortal memory
Floating in a basket along the Nile
Drifting into reeds near the shore
Three women reach with a smile
Holding me with love
All I wanted was more

A Terza Rima for Passover

What kind of man was this Moses?
Did he know all along how his life would unfold?
Here is the secret that Passover shows us:

From orphan, to aristocrat, then back in the cold
Wandering the desert, he settles down in modesty
Then God calls on him to lead and break the mold

Only when he was humble enough to accept God's plan
If we quiet our minds, listen to our heart, then God speaks
That's when each of us has the potential to be the Great Man

Art is About Making the Invisible Visible

Art can be political in that it educates us about invisible people—making us more empathetic to those who remain invisible.

Art can be about making the transcendental visible.

Art can be about making music visible.

Bright, Pure Colors

Bright, pure colors are characteristic
  of the Other World

Bright pure colors are the essence of
  A Special Kind of Beauty

  That of the visionary

  As usual first was Plato
      then Acquinas
          later Huxley

  How did Rothko know?
          Did he talk to Ellsworth Kelly?
Matisse was way before and far away

Did James Turrell talk with Plato at a Quaker meeting?
  Did Dan Flavin have an espresso with Monet?

    Bright
        Pure
            Colors

    Each
        Visionary
            Brothers

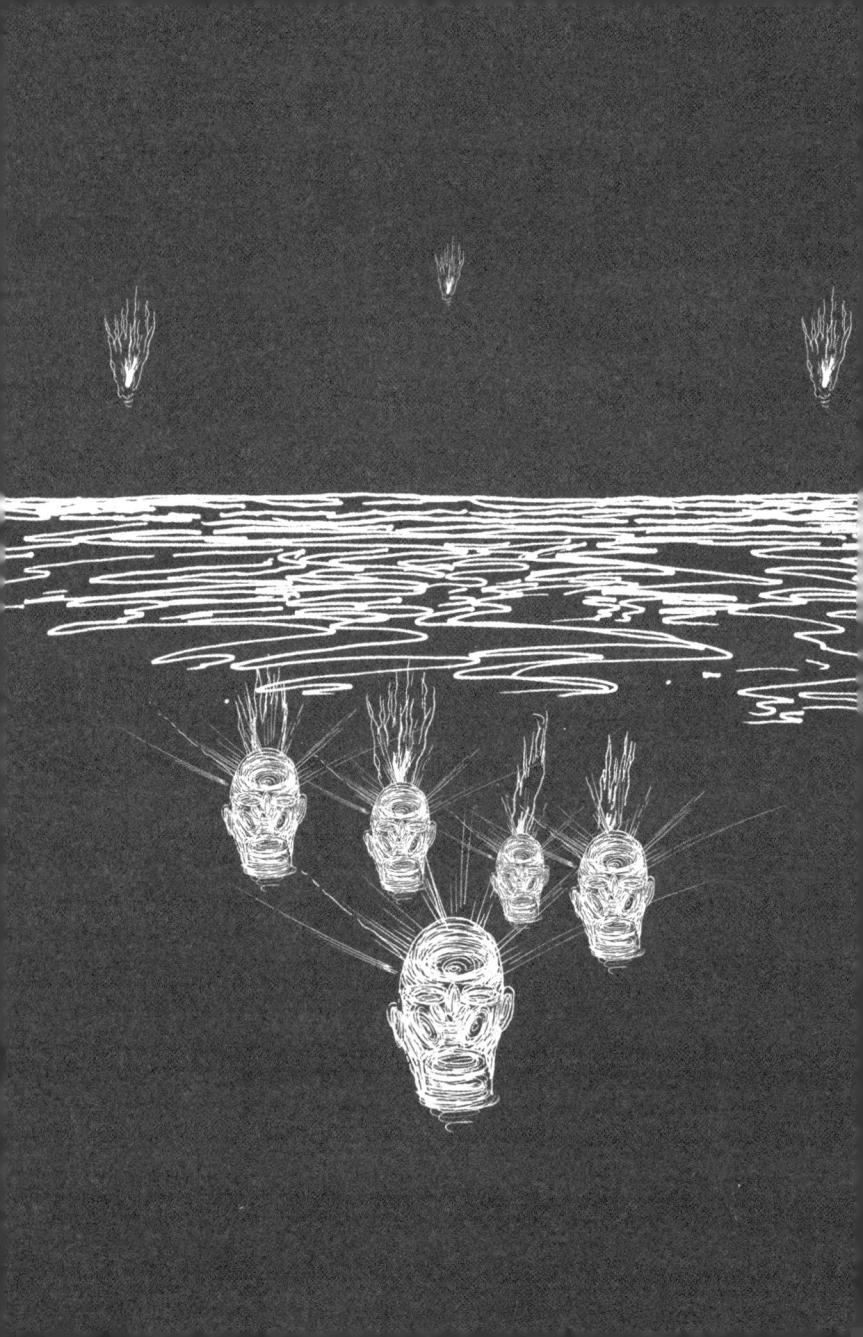

It's All the Same

Kabbalah
Taoism
LSD magic musrooms
Buddha
Ram Dass

mescaline ayahuasca
are all just doors
all lead to the same
place space truth
a seminar table
the vase in the center
is glowing Truth
around the seminar table sit
Lao Tzu, Socrates, Plato,
Siddhartha, Shakespeare,
Isaac Luria, Aristotle, Freud,
Jesus, Moses, Pythagoras, Mozart
Einstein, Albert Hofman, Aldous Huxley
all of them sitting around chatting
all of them just an angle
a vertex
all angles leading
to one single

Point

Euclid was right about the Point
Chatting, maybe smoking, laughing

Bach is in the corner playing softly on his harpsichord
THAT is the room where it happens. . .

Jacob's Ladder—
A New Dream Interpretation

I dreamt a

      L
      A
      D
      D
      E
      R

          super tall and thin
          rising up to the sky

            precarious

I was seeing the drama unfold from a close distance
    I was floating in the ocean

The problem was the base
      The base of the ladder was in the ocean

People were swimming intently toward it and they began to

      C
      L
      I
      M
      B

People swimming up to the ladder,
then beginning their climb
Like those photos of the traffic jam
of climbers
                               on Mount Everest

the mountain overrun by finance bros paying sherpas to carry their egos

A long line of strivers
I am shaking my head and muttering to myself,
"can't they see?"
                 there is no solid base
                 there are no solid supports
                 the ladder is just floating in the sea.
The weight of all the people climbing begins the inevitable

                 T
               I
                   L
                   T

The Ladder falls backward in the sea
Then the bodies are all piled up on dry land
                       I walk between them

For those who I can see had Love in them
and I place a loving hand on their bodies
You can't climb that ladder without a solid base of . . .
God, humility, love, family, and community holding the
base of the ladder

Actually. . . I think the ladder leads to nowhere anyway.
        Better to have awareness that the climbing is mindless
              Mindless climbing
              Stop climbing
              Stop climbing

                I shout out,
          "Guys, God is right here in the ocean."

More Social, Less Media

More IRL—In Real Life

Face-to-face interactions need to be the next new/old thing.

Alien Cinquain

Big eyes
Huge oval head
Am I an alien?
In ancient Egypt we arrived
To teach.

On China

In the West, we are ignorant of the wisdom of the East.

If we have any hope of diffusing this Cold War with China, our leaders (and our citizens who elect our leaders) should start by reading some Lao Tzu and Confucius.

Iceland Haiku

Floating in hot spring

Northern lights dazzle my soul

Eyes water with joy.

Mozart

Mozart said that he never wrote anything; he was just a vessel transcribing for God. Wolfgang "Amadeus" Mozart. Amadeus means "Beloved of God."

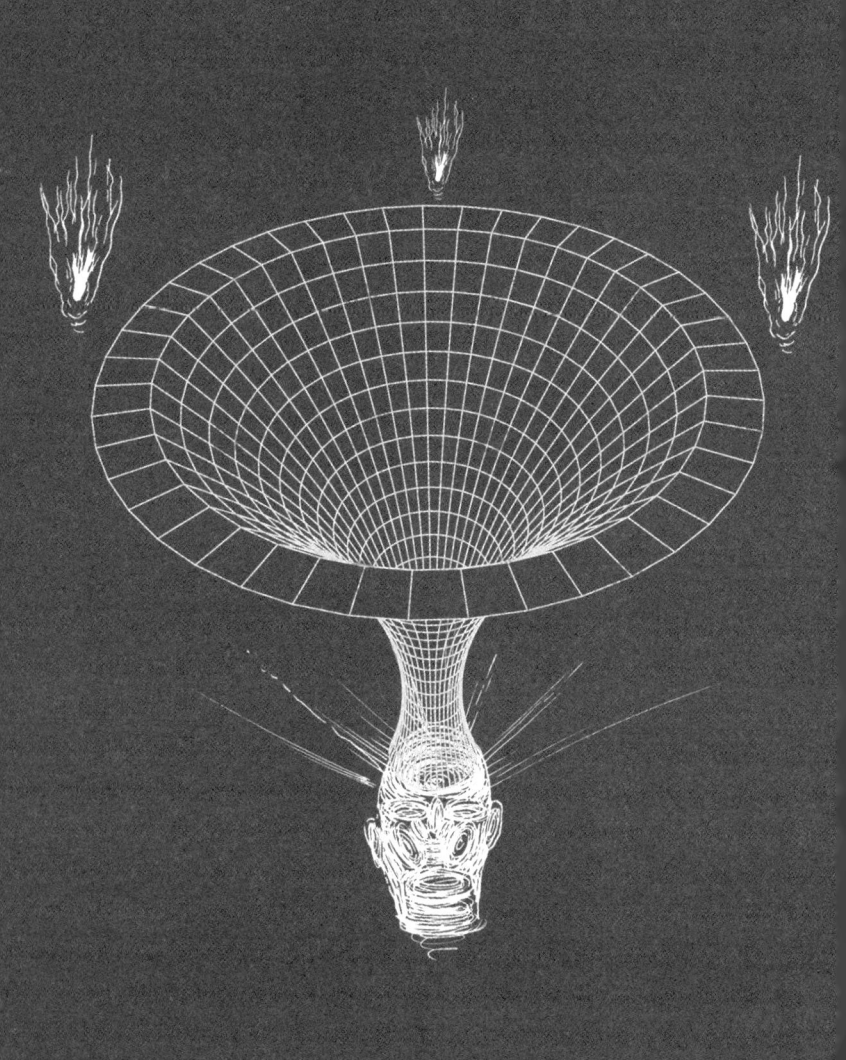

The 1% Versus the 99%

Kabbalah teaches that we live our lives in the 1% of Reality. There is an Ocean of Reality around us—the 99%.

The human brain evolved in such a way where its primary purpose is to act like a filter at the bottom of a little drain at the bottom of the infinite Ocean of Reality. There is so much energy, love, joy, and paradox involved with the Ocean of Reality/Truth that our brains cannot handle it. We need our brains to be focused on the day-to-day realities of the survival of our bodies. Therefore, our brains are built to funnel all of that down into just a few drips. Each drip is a memory of the Truth of the 99% Ocean.

There are various methods that can allow the filter of our brains to open up more and our souls can temporarily swim like joyous dolphins in that Ocean.

Koreshika-Nai

The Japanese saying "koreshika-nai" means there is only one way to do it... the perfect way.

This is True.

The art of the Japanese tea ceremony is koreshika-nai in poetic action.

The Death of Simple Curiosity

An excessive amount of information in the field of consciousness (Infosphere) is overwhelming and is causing a giving up on simple curiosity. People are no longer curious about what they can learn from another person and they stop asking questions in conversation. When we cease to be curious about one another, everyone feels unseen.

Things That Are True

What can you still count on in the postmodern relativist world?

This is what I have deduced to be absolutely true regardless of place, time, and social circumstance.

- All humans just want Unconditional Love.

- The answer is always Radical Vulnerability.

- Never waste an opportunity to make someone laugh and smile.

- Death and Life, Dark and Light, Fear and Love. It's all ONE.

- Every two hours, stop and do a random act of Love.

- All the religions and spiritual teachings are just various pathways to the same Truth.

- Since we are all just walking each other Home, it is utterly ridiculous to be at war with one another.

In Praise of Conversation

Intellectually and culturally we just bounce around like random billiard balls, reacting to the latest random stimuli.

—Jonathan Franzen, *Freedom*

People are mistaking enhanced, speedy communication—which could be grunts or text acronyms like "SRY" for "Sorry"—for actual conversation.

Conversation requires training and practice—something our education system mostly overlooks in favor of testing facts which will soon be outdated or not unnecessary to know because technology will provide instant access to all facts.

Can technology balance reason, passion, beauty, and justice? I say emphatically, no. It never will. Even AI will not comprehend passion or beauty.

How do we make it pleasurable and desirable for people to want to engage in conversation where their beliefs may be shown to be false or indefensible? That is usually quite uncomfortable.

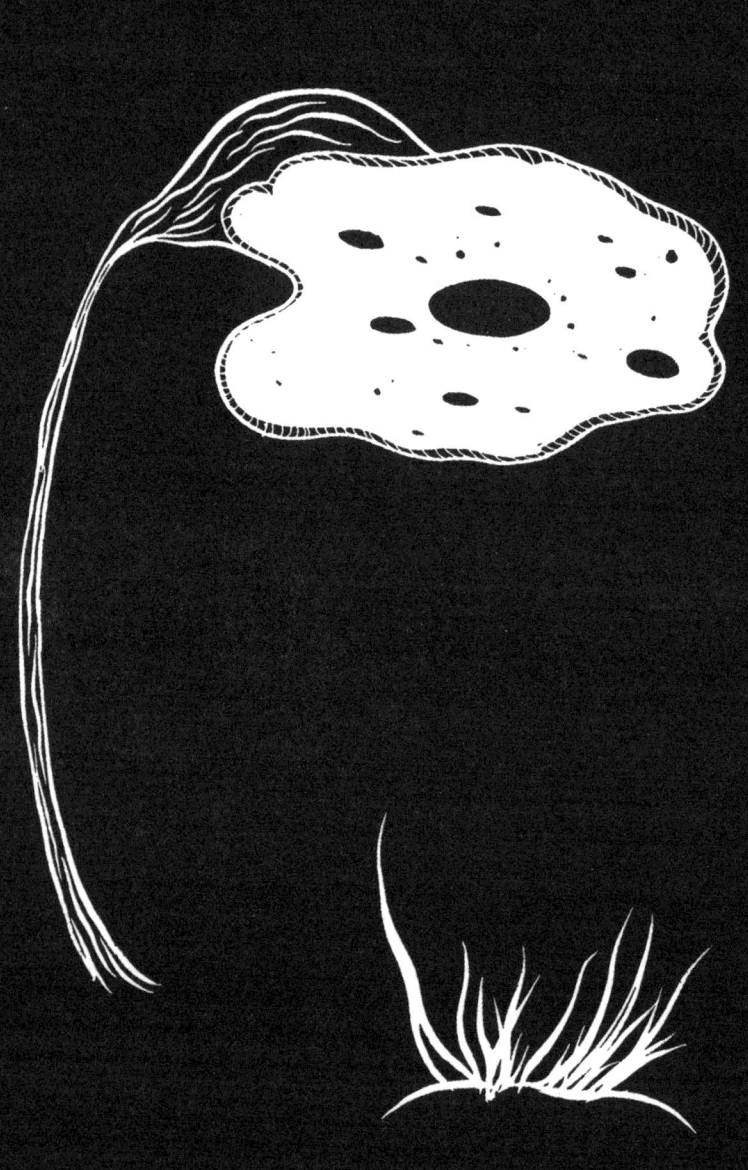

God doesn't really talk,

He communicates in music.

He doesn't send a meeting invite.

God doesn't use Outlook.

Lunatic

Definition—Someone who is keenly aware of and influenced by the power of the moon (lunar) cycles.

If only more humans were lunatics.

We have become so far removed from the power and wisdom of primitive nature.

Lunatics are those who are wise and tuned into nature.

Those of us who are slaves to our technology are the sick ones.

Poetry can point us toward
the door where Truth lies
and then stands aside, allowing us to enter.
While prose stands in the doorway
and tries to describe the wonders
on the other side,
but rarely lets us pass through.

—Adrienne Rich

If Everyone Just Took the Right Dose of Psychedelics

Then everyone would have clarity.

Everyone would see themselves accurately and see the world from above, just as I am describing it to you.

If there is one piece of advice you take from this book, it should be to go do a proper, medically supervised psychedelic/entheogenic plant medicine journey for yourself.

This will heal the world.

Answer Society

We are an answer society, not a question society.

Everyone wants their reward (cookie or gold star) for the right answer.

We don't value good questions.

Try to keep track of how many times a person uses
"I, me, my" when they speak.
That will tell you how evolved their soul is.

God is Energy

God is ceaseless energy
Animating force
All language is merely symbolic
Words fail
Words are just symbols and metaphors of the actual reality
Words, paintings, physics formulas…
All are just symbolically pointing in the direction
Of reality, of the truth
Aristotle was onto it to name God as the "Prime Mover"
Lucretius was onto it by naming God "the Swerve"
Lao Tzu was onto it when he kept comparing the Tao
to the movement of water
Alan Watts accurately summed it up in *The Wisdom of Insecurity*
"There is no past or future…only a series of nows "
Einstein tried to quantify God with $E = mc^2$
We are also part of God
We are nothing more than energy
We are each a frequency
Vibration
Energy
There is no "I" and there is no separate "God"
It's all us
It's all now.

The Act of Creation

The act of creation is always a risk.
But it's always a risk worth taking.
When we create, we are like God.
And since we are each a part of God,
Creating is just being ourselves!

If we don't create
The universe stands still
Atrophy
If you don't create
You are standing still
Dying
Creation is dynamism.
And that is the fire of life.

Create a company. It may fail.
Write a poem. It might suck.
Make a film. It may never be a hit.
Build a boat. It may sink.
Bring a child into the world. It may die.

But what would life be if we didn't have the
courage to take these risks?

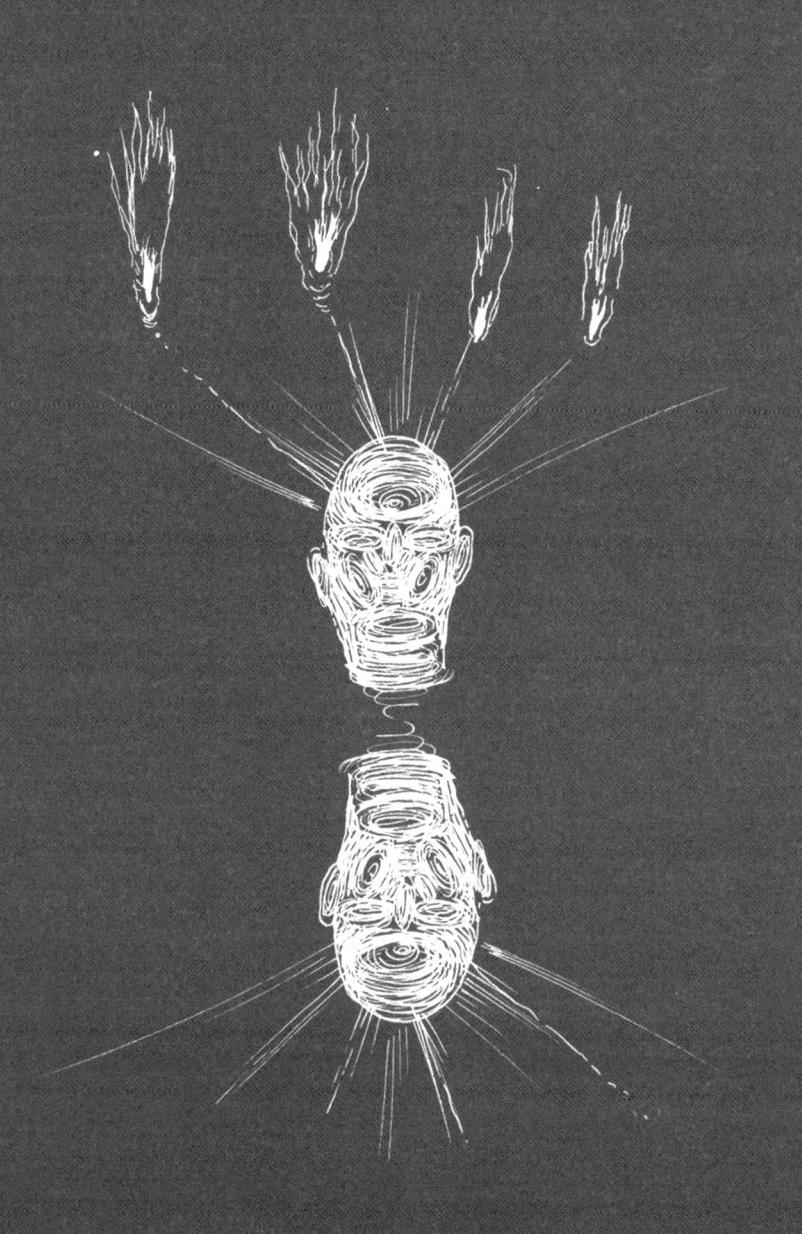

On the Breakdown of the Family Unit

Families are all dispersing.

Kids are so busy with sports and activities that there is no actual connection with family and friends.

Too much structured activity for kids leads them to not learn how to be imaginative, how to play, how to resolve conflict amongst other kids.

The collapse of family dinners and real family discussions will be the collapse of civilization.

All politics starts with the family unit. If family units are sick, our politics will be sick.

Children who are overly reliant on parents to issue commands will become adults who are desirous of tyrants and authoritarian governments to issue commands.

Communities, packs, tribes—this is how humans are meant to organize themselves.

When we splinter apart into individual atoms, we are not only alone, we are out of sync with our fundamental nature.

Humans need to stop traveling so much. Humans need less freedom of movement right now.

We need to learn to sit still and get reconnected again with our families, our tribes, our communities.

Throw away the phones and ground the planes.

Don't Squeeze

Don't hold on to life so tightly.
I'll squeeze the life out of myself.
Hold on to life lightly!
Like holding a dove
Or placing a Ming vase on a shelf.

On Charity

The true purpose of charity is to give of ourselves to our fellow mankind who are in need of help and love.

While I want to be cautious not to be too harsh on all charitable organizations, the inherent problem with formal organizations is the inevitability that institutions of all sorts (governments, religious institutions, private clubs, etc.) eventually, and sometimes unintentionally, become primarily focused on the self-perpetuation of the institution itself because the institution has become a sort of jobs program. If one looks at the financials of most charities, you will find that most of the money that comes in goes to financing the jobs of the people who work there and the administrative overhead of the institution. An unfortunately small percentage of the donations actually go to those in need of charity. Institutions seek to perpetuate themselves first and foremost. One need look no further than the Vatican and ask about how much charity was retained by the institution versus how much actually went to those in need.

If you look closely at the life of Jesus of Nazareth, we find that his charity and ministry were very much person-to-person. There was very little administrative overhead in his ministry. For him, it was all about talking to, healing, and giving to people, one person at a time.

Another important aspect of charity is the positive effect it can have on the soul of the giver. Charity is a two-way street. It's just as important for the giver to feel the benefits of giving his time, treasure, and attention to another soul as it is for the recipient to feel the generosity and love of his fellow man.

When I make a donation to a large charitable institution, I

have found that my soul does not light up in the same way it does when I give time or treasure directly to a random human in need that I encounter on the street. The interaction and the conversation with another person, the direct smile, and the heartfelt "thank you" from the recipient really light up the soul of the giver.

Therefore, I submit to you that the proper way to be charitable is to:

1. Volunteer your time and personally go help another person with your own hands and your own good spirit. Beam your love into another person.

2. Determine your financial budget for how much money you want to give to others in need. Then, each week, withdraw the budgeted amount of cash and walk around your town every week and personally give the money away to random people in need. Talk to them and wish them well. Pay attention to how good you feel doing this.

3. Everything needs to be done face-to-face in order to really experience the true benefits of charity.

4. Just sending in a check to a charitable institution is another form of disconnection, abstraction, and alienation from yourself and your fellow humans.

The Problem is Not

The problem is not that we don't know how to live...

The problem is that we don't know how to read.

The problem is that with each successive generation, increasingly few people actually read all the wisdom that has already been written down.

This is the ironic and cruel tragedy of today's world:

All of the answers and
all the happiness we seek...
are directly in front of us!
Peace and prosperity are right in front of us.
Truth and Beauty are right in front of us.
It's all there at your local library
and the local bookstore.
And yet the humans would rather spend
$8,000 on a ticket to see Taylor Swift
and bury their faces swiping through Tik Tok videos
of French bull dogs who skateboard.
And they claim they are too busy
to read or to know anything about Hannah Arendt.

I just shake my head
in resignation.
It's a crying fucking shame.
When Jesus asked God to forgive them
while he was pinned up on the Cross
"For they know not what they do God!!"
At what point, God do you just say. . .
they are so fucking stupid.

let them destroy themselves
while listening to their Taylor Swift song
"Blank Space,"
which is an apt description
for the space between their ears.

Random Morning Satori

- Why must learning for learning's sake be justified?

- There is such profound resignation when we assume that the masses are only capable of being trained to perform some practical "job" and nothing higher.

- There is no understanding by assuming one knows anything from just one word or one headline. I find most people confuse knowledge with scanning many headlines. Eventually one must realize that wisdom cannot be found in headlines or CliffsNotes. You must read in-depth.

- Poetry is a privilege.

- When one encounters a soul that is in tremendous pain and profound ignorance, you must try to accept and embrace the spiritual challenge to somehow find the mercy and compassion for this struggling soul, despite how ugly they present themselves.

Forms of Capital

There are more forms of capital than just money.

Social
Political
Intellectual
Cultural

Warrior Poet

maybe i am a warrior

a warrior for soul
a warrior for inquiry
a warrior for books
a warrior for wisdom
a warrior for seeking
a warrior for reason
a warrior for listening
a warrior for intuition
a warrior for the arts
a warrior for the humanities
a warrior for remembrance
a warrior for studying
a warrior for discourse
a warrior for the seminar table
a warrior for mother earth

maybe the world needs warrior poets

Is Poetry Dead?

Even a strong tree loses all its leaves
for a season
but it stays alive through the winter.

Even those who no longer read
nor care to study
quote from Psalms all the time.

Even the most selfish country
that has ever existed
has a faint memory of its true national anthem:
"Song of Myself."

Even in the Dark Ages
(then and now)
poetry vibrates in the soul of humans.

Each new epoch of human advancement
has been kicked off
by an Epic Poem.

So no, poetry is not dead.
Now is just a winter of the intellect and the heart.
I see green shoots of poetry in the souls of our children.

Golfing with Maharajji

I had a dream that I was playing golf and Neem Karoli Baba was my caddy. I am playing well and feeling confident, but the greens on this course are comically difficult. One green is so small and is on top of a super tall skinny pillar of grass stretching up high in the sky like a Dr. Suess drawing. I hit a terrific drive three hundred yards down the middle of the fairway. Maharajji claps and we walk. I hit a good approach shot to this ridiculously high, tiny green, but it's impossible to stop the ball on the green; it is so small. I turn to Baba after I hit the shot, and he is laughing at me. I'm frustrated. I can't tell if I should laugh too or if his laughing at me suggests I'm not skilled enough or good enough to hit that shot. The only positive thing is that I do not feel abandoned or rejected by him. I have to rethink: why would I play the game in the normal way with such a silly, impossible green to hit? I am no master.

אֱמֶת Truth

Aleph is the first letter of the Hebrew alphabet. Mem is the exact middle letter of the alphabet. Tav is the last letter of the alphabet.

Therefore, the "Truth" is spelled out (is encompassed) by the beginning, the middle, and the end of the alphabet itself.

Gematria is a method of interpretation that involves calculating numerical values to words and names. The method is used in mystical interpretations of Scripture. Think Bible codes.

Aleph = 1

Mem = 40

Tav = 400

אֱמֶת Truth = 441

The Mispar Katan (sum of the integers or literally "small number") of Truth = 9 [4 + 4 + 1 = 9]

9 is the final numeral symbolizing completeness and total wisdom.

9 is also the only numeral where all of its multiples have a "Mispar Katan" of 9 itself. For example:

9 x 2 = 18 (Mispar Katan of 18 is 1 +8 = 9)

9 x 3 = 27 (Mispar Katan of 27 is 2 + 7 = 9)

9 x 4 = 36 (Mispar Katan of 36 is 3 + 6 = 9)

and so on

9 is the complete number.

Truth nine complete wisdom everything all-encompassing Truth.

This is God's secret "signature" that there is meaning in the universe. Math is giving us meaning.

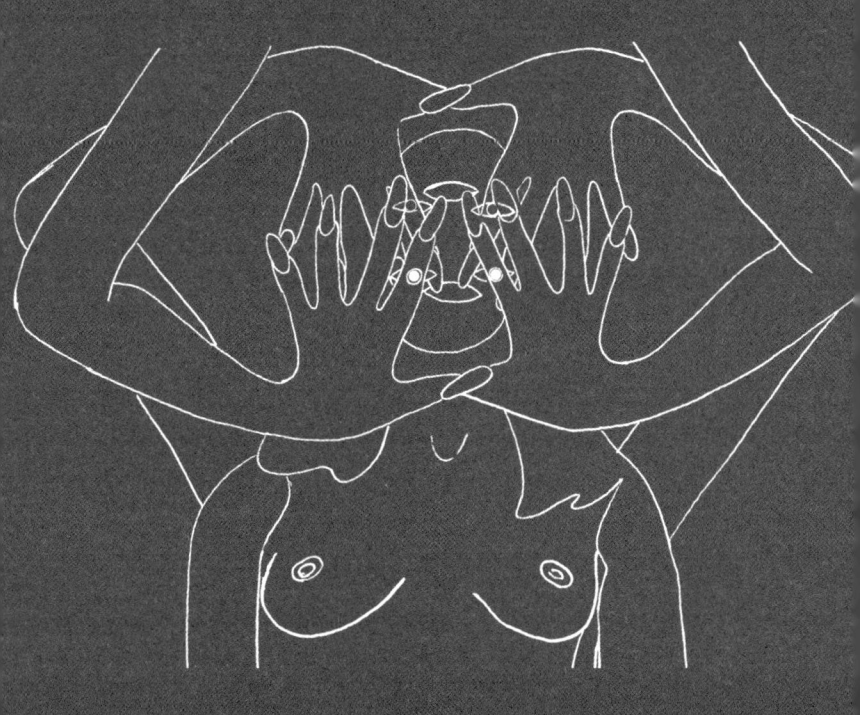

The Trumpet of Joshua

Joshua blew the walls of Jericho down.
How does one blow down the walls of ignorance today?
There is no shortage of shouting
And outrage
On our scrolling feeds.

Perhaps poetry can be the trumpet
Of today and tomorrow?
Perhaps ecstatic painting
Can be the banner of the conqueror?

I call for a renaissance of the human arts!
What the world needs now is more artists
And philosophers and songwriters and poets!
Give me the quiet and skilled folk music
Of the "Milk Carton Kids"—
Not the STEM kids.
Give me the spiritual paintings of Hilma af Klint!
Not the AI-generated shadows of DALL-E!

"Do not be frightened,
And do not be dismayed"[1]
For the poets of a new age are among us.
Hear my trumpet call!
Save us from ourselves!
Remind us of what it means to be human.

---

[1] Joshua 1:9

A Renaissance of Humanism

An "Alienist" (a.k.a. a psychologist, according to Marx) is a person who helps people get reconnected to life. An "Alienist" is a healer of humans from alienation. Marx foresaw that we need authentic community to (re)find our humanity. Marx posited that "alienation" from our humanity was caused by the technological isolation brought on by the Industrial Revolution. Once again, at the turn of another century, we are in the same place again.

Technology is a tool, not something you live inside of. It is critical that the youth understand the difference.

We have lost direct connection with real life.

Today, we need spiritual aerobics. Just as we now go to workout classes to compensate for the fact that technology makes it so we don't need to chop wood and carry water. So too must we now compensate for our actual loss of human connection and conversation.

It is more incumbent on us to reach out to others for real physical human connection.

Social media is the illusion of connection.

I call for a renaissance of humanism! We must read and talk and listen to each other face-to-face! Technology is the enemy!

We have become so siloed that there is no space for real conversation and real listening—the answer is the monastery of learning.

Kusunoki Masashige

Poet Warrior
Artist Samurai
Father General
Sage Rage
Beauty Blood
Calm Frenzy
Lover Killer
Flute Screams
Zen War

AH! The Peonies!
The painting
Cy Twombly
The Lesson:
The Necessity of Art:
We all must take off our armor forevermore.

On Fear

"How do I block the fear?" Du Fu[1] answers: "How does a tree block the wind?"

You don't resist the fear; you let it run through you. Surf the fear.

[1] Du Fu — Chinese Poet 712-770 A.D.

The Question

In my dream, I sat in front of Maharajji's tucket, rubbing his feet.

He smiled at me with a smile that combined love with mocking.

He took out a large blue notecard from under his blanket and started writing...

He then held up the card to me with that smile on his face.

The card read:

"In this lifetime, can you renounce money, power, and sexual desire?"

He said nothing, but spoke directly into my mind,

"If yes, then you are done with reincarnation."

"If yes, you may have siddhi powers."

Psychedelic Psalms by Joshua Dean Rogers
First North American Edition, 2024
Copyright © 2024 by Hat & Beard Press, Los Angeles
All rights reserved.

Except for select photographs authorized for press and promotion, no part of this book may be reproduced in any form by any means, electronic or mechanical, including photocopying and recording, or by any information storage and retrieval system, without permission in writing from the publisher.

ISBN 978-1-955125-32-9
10 9 8 7 6 5 4 3 2 1

Cover Design by Mariano Chavez
Book Design by Sabrina Che
Copyright © Joshua Dean Rogers
Printed in Slovenia by Oddi

Illustrations by Mariano Chavez
Edited by J.C Gabel, Sybil Perez, and John Tottenham

This book was produced in partnership with Invisible Republic, an arts nonprofit and programming initiative of Future Roots, Inc., a 501c3 organization.

Hat & Beard Press books are published by
Hat & Beard, LLC
713 N La Fayette Park Place
Los Angeles, CA 90026

www.hatandbeard.com
IG: @hatandbeardpress

HAT & BEARD PRESS   **INVISIBLE REPUBLIC**